DIFFICULT RIDDLES
FOR SMART KIDS

300 RIDDLES AND BRAIN TEASERS
THAT KIDS AND FAMILIES WILL LOVE

M. PREFONTAINE

CONTENTS

INTRODUCTION

"The mind once stretched by a new idea, never returns to its original dimensions."

Ralph Waldo Emerson

This book is a collection of 300 brain teasing riddles and puzzles. Their purpose is to make children think and stretch the mind. They are designed to test logic, lateral thinking as well as memory and to engage the brain in seeing patterns and connections between different things and circumstances.

They are laid out in three chapters which get more difficult as you go through the book, in the author's opinion at least. The answers are at the back of the book if all else fails.

These are more difficult riddles and are designed to be attempted by children from 10 years onwards, as well as participation from the rest of the family.

DIFFICULT RIDDLES

1. When you do not know what I am, then I am something. But when you know what I am, then I am nothing. What am I?

2. You can see me in water, but I never get wet. What am I?

3. The more you take, the more you leave behind. What am I?

4. When I am released to the wind, you look away and you pretend, but away your friends I will send. What am I?

5. What English word has three consecutive double letters?

6. Imagine you are in a dark room. How do you get out?

7. What English word retains the same pronunciation, even after you take away four of its five letters?

8. When you have me, you feel like sharing me. But, if you do share me, you don't have me. What am I?

9. A man is pushing his car along the road when he comes to a hotel. He shouts, "I'm bankrupt!" Why?

10. An English word has six letters, remove one letter, and twelve remains. What am I?

11. What question can you never answer yes to?

12. What invention lets you look right through a wall?

13. What is as light as a feather, but even the world's strongest man couldn't hold it for more than a minute?

14. What occurs once in every minute, twice in every moment, yet never in a thousand years?

15. I never ask questions but am always answered. What am I?

16. If you go to the movies and you're paying, is it cheaper to take one friend to the movies twice, or two friends to the movies at the same time?

17. What gets bigger every time you take from it?

18. What is full of holes, but can still hold a lot of water?

19. Which came first the chicken or the egg?

20. No matter how much rain comes down on it, it won't get any wetter. What is it?

21. I'm flat when I'm new. I'm fat when you use me. I release my gas when something sharp touches me. What am I?

22. Three times what number is no larger than two times that same number?

23. What do you throw out when you want to use it, but take in when you don't want to use it?

24. I cannot hear or even see, but sense light and sounds that may be. Sometimes I end up on the hook, or even deep into a book. What am I?

25. Which ring is square?

26. Why are manholes round instead of square?

27. What tastes better than it smells?

28. At night, they come without being fetched. By day they are lost without being stolen. What are they?

29. The more you have of it, the less you see. What is it?

30. What starts with a T, ends with a T, and has T in it?

31. Say my name and I disappear. What am I?

32. What is it that after you take away the whole, some still remains?

33. Forward I'm heavy, but backwards I'm not. What am I?

34. I am a box that holds keys without locks, yet they can unlock your soul. What am I?

35. My first is twice in apple but not once in tart. My second is in liver but not in heart. My third is in giant and also in ghost. Whole I'm best when I am roast. What am I?

36. Remove six letters from this sequence to reveal a familiar English word.
BSAINXLEATNTEARS

37. What has four wheels and flies?

38. What has a forest but no trees, cities but no people and rivers but no water?

39. Runs smoother than any rhyme, loves to fall but cannot climb. What am I?

40. Take me and scratch my head. What once was red, is black instead. What am I?

41. What is as big as you are and yet does not weigh anything?

42. It is an insect, and the first part of its name is the name of another insect. What is it?

43. I'm where yesterday follows today, and tomorrow's in the middle. What am I?

44. How much dirt is there in a hole 3 feet deep, 6 ft. long and 4 ft. wide?

45. Name all the numbers from 1 – 100, which have the letter 'A' in their spellings?

46. What kind of coat is always wet when you put it on?

47. What kind of cheese is made backwards?

48. What can you hold in your right hand but never in your left hand?

49. During what month do people sleep the least?

50. What can never be placed in a sauce pan?

51. I am always there, some distance away, somewhere between land or sea and sky I lay. You may move towards me, but distant I will stay. What am I?

52. I can only live where there is light, but I die if the light shines on me. What am I?

53. What kind of room has no doors or windows?

54. What can you catch but not throw?

55. What has a heart but no other organs?

56. Two people are born at the same moment, but they don't have the same birthdays. How could this be?

57. What's orange and sounds like a parrot?

58. What always goes to bed with its shoes on?

59. How can you make 7 even?

60. What am I?

61. I can bring tears to your eyes; resurrect the dead, make you smile, and reverse time. I form in an instant but I last a lifetime. What am I?

62. Mr. Smith has two children. If the older child is a boy, what are the odds that the other child is also a boy?

63. A man builds a house rectangular in shape. All the sides have southern exposure. A big bear walks by. What color is the bear? Why?

64. What starts with an e but only has a single letter in it?

65. A girl who was just learning to drive went down a one-way street in the wrong direction, but didn't break the law. How come?

66. If in a car race, the man who came two places in front of the last man finished one ahead of the man who came fifth. How many contestants were there?

67. A murderer is condemned to death. He has to choose between three rooms. The first is full of raging fires, the second is full of assassins with loaded guns, and the third is full of lions that haven't eaten in 3 years. Which room is safest for him?

68. What's black and white and red all over?

69. What flies when it's born, lies when it's alive, and runs when it's dead?

70. I am the only organ that named myself. What am I?

71. You walk into a room with a rabbit holding a carrot, a pig eating slop, and a chimp holding a banana. Which animal in the room is the smartest?

72. What always murmurs but never talks, always runs but never walks, has a bed but never sleeps, has a mouth but never speaks?

73. I am taken from a mine, and shut up in a wooden case, from which I am never released, and yet I am used by almost everybody. What am I?

74. I'm tall when I'm young and I'm short when I'm old. What am I?

75. What house can fly?

76. What goes up and doesn't go down?

77. No matter how terrible things get for the people of the Arctic, they will not eat a penguin. Why?

78. A group of ten people are going out for pizza but only two of them have an umbrella to keep them dry. But they manage to walk all the way to the pizza place without getting wet. How is this possible?

79. What runs around the house but doesn't move?

80. What goes around the house and in the house but never touches the house?

81. A man finds a small iron coin dated 154 B.C., what's it worth?

82. There is a one-story house. The walls are blue, the floor is pink, the stove and cupboards are red. What color are the stairs?

83. Why was the baby strawberry crying?

84. I can be cracked; I can be made. I can be told; I can be played. What am I?

85. I can't go left; I can't go right. I am forever stuck in a building over three stories high. What am I?

86. What goes back and forth constantly, but never in a straight line?

87. What dress can you not wear?

88. What belongs to you but others use it more?

89. I don't have eyes, but once I did see. Once I had thought, but am now white and empty. What am I?

90. What has hands that can't clap?

91. Which three numbers have the same answer when added together and multiplied together?

92. What has a mouth but can't chew?

93. How did Mark legally marry three women in Michigan, without divorcing any of them, becoming legally separated, or any of them dying?

94. I have all the knowledge you have. But I am not much larger than your fist. What am I?

95. Everyone in the world needs it. They generously give it, but rarely take it. What is it?

96. Take off my skin - I won't cry, but you will. What am I?

97. Lighter than what I am made of, more of me is hidden than is seen. What am I?

98. You heard me before, yet you hear me again, then I die 'till you call me again. What am I?

99. If you were standing directly on Antarctica's South Pole facing north, which direction would you travel if you took one step backward?

100. What has a neck but no head?

101. Two girls were born to the same mother, on the same day, at the same time, in the same month and year and yet they're not twins. How can this be?

102. Rearrange all the letters in the sentence to form a well-known proverb.
"I don't admit women are faint."

103. A woman was sitting in her hotel room when there was a knock at the door. She opened the door to see a man whom she had never seen before. He said "oh I'm sorry, I have made a mistake, I thought this was my room." He then went down the corridor and in the elevator. The woman went back into her room and phoned security. What made the woman so suspicious of the man?

104. How can you physically stand behind your father while he is standing behind you?

105. I have an eye but I am blind, a sea, but no water; a bee, but no honey; tea but no coffee; and a why, but no answer. What am I?

106. What 4-letter word can be written forward, backward or upside down, and can still be read from left to right?

107. Pronounced as one letter, and written with three, two letters there are, and two only in me. I'm double, I'm single, I'm black, blue, and gray, I'm read from both ends, and the same either way. What am I?

108. Rearrange all the letters in this sentence to form a well-known proverb.
"The broad flag of the free. It rocks."

109. What common English verb becomes its own past tense by rearranging its letters?

110. What has cities, but no houses; forests, but no trees; and water, but no fish?

111. Who is it that rows quickly with four oars but never comes out from under his own roof?

112. You hear it speak, for it has a hard tongue. But it cannot breathe, for it has not a lung. What is it?

113. What are the next 3 letters in this riddle? o t t f f s s...

114. Rearrange all the letters in this sentence to form a well-known proverb.
"Strong lions share almost gone."

115. I'm a word that's hardly there. Take away my start, and I'm an herb. What am I?

116. The one who makes it, sells it. The one who buys it, never uses it. The one that uses it never knows that he's using it. What is it?

117. A box without hinges, lock or key, yet golden treasure lies within. What is it?

118. What has a neck and no head, two arms but no hands?

119. I am a word of 5 letters and people eat me. If you remove the first letter, I become a form of energy. Remove the first two and I'm needed to live. Scramble the last 3 and you can drink me. What am I?

120. Alive without breath, as cold as death, clad in mail never clinking, never thirsty and ever drinking. What am I?

121. We are five little objects of an everyday sort; you will find us all in the ladies' court. What are we?

122. Blend a 'teapot shot' so the pearlies won't rot. What am I?

123. Always invisible, yet never out of sight. What are they?

124. A beggar's brother died, but the man who died had no brother. How could this be?

125. I stand when I'm sitting, and jump when I'm walking. Who am I?

126. What has a tongue, cannot walk, but gets around a lot?

127. What has no beginning, end, or middle?

128. On my way to St. Ives I saw a man with 7 wives. Each wife had 7 sacks. Each sack had 7 cats. Each cat had 7 kittens. Kittens, cats, sacks, wives. How many were going to St. Ives?

129. A little girl kicks a soccer ball. It goes 10 feet away from her and then comes back to her. How is this possible?

130. A 10-foot rope ladder hangs over the side of a boat with the bottom rung on the surface of the water. The rungs are one foot apart, and the tide goes up at the rate of 6 inches per hour. How long will it be until three rungs are covered?

131. A is the father of B. But B is not the son of A. How's that possible?

132. What can fill an entire room without taking up any space?

133. You throw away the outside, eat the inside and throw away the inside. What am I?

134. Take me for a spin and I will make you cool, use me in winter and you are a fool. What am I?

135. Where can you finish a book without finishing a sentence?

136. It cannot be seen, cannot be felt, cannot be heard, cannot be smelt. It lies behind stars and under hills, and empty holes it fills. It comes first and follows, ends life, kills laughter. What am I?

137. This thing all things devours: birds, beasts, trees, flowers; gnaws iron, bites steel; grinds hard stones to meal; slays kings, ruins towns, and beats high mountains down. What am I?

138. I am a seed with three letters in my name. Take away the last two and I still sound the same. What am I?

139. People buy me to eat, but never eat me. What am I?

140. What's made of wood but can't be sawed?

141. What number do you get when you multiply all of the numbers on a telephone's number pad?

142. Arrange four nines and a one and only one mathematical symbol to make it equal to 100.

143. When you look for something, why is it always in the last place you look?

144. You use me from your head to your toes, the more I work the thinner I grow. What am I?

145. I am a cold man without a soul. If there is warmth in me, it slowly will kill me. What am I?

146. I stare at you; you stare at me. I have three eyes, yet can't see. Every time I blink, I give you commands. You do as you are told, with your feet and hands. What am I?

147. How do you make the number one disappear by adding to it?

148. An empty bus pulls up to a stop and 10 people get on. At the next stop 5 people get off and twice as many people get on as at the first stop. At the third stop 25 get off. How many people are on the bus at this point?

149. 100 feet in the air, yet my back is on the ground. What am I?

150. A king, queen, and two twins all lay in a large room. How are there no adults in the room?

151. There is a window cleaner who is cleaning a window on the 25th floor of a skyscraper. He suddenly slips and falls. He has no safety equipment and nothing to soften his fall, but he is not hurt at all. How do you account for that?

152. What is bought by the yard but is worn by the foot?

153. The more places I be, the less you can see. What am I?

154. I am an instrument that you can hear, but you cannot touch or see me. What am I?

155. What table can you eat?

156. What demands an answer, but asks no question?

157. What sport starts with a T, has four letters, and is played around the world?

158. There are two planes. One is going from New York to London at a speed of 600 MPH. The other is traveling from London to New York at a speed of 500 MPH. When the planes meet which one will be closer to London?

159. You have a large number of friends coming over and they all get thirsty. Your first friend asks for 1/2 a cup of water. Your second friend asks for 1/4 a cup of water. Your third friend asks for 1/8 a cup of water, etc. How many cups of water do you need to serve your friends?

160. There are 50 crows on a wire. A hunter shoots and kills three. How many crows are left on the wire?

161. What is 40 divided by 1/2, plus 15?

162. A man is sitting in his cabin in Michigan. 3 hours later he gets out of his cabin in Texas. How is this possible?

163. When angry I turn red, cold I turn blue and pale when scared. What am I?

164. I have two arms, but fingers I have none. I've got two feet, but I cannot run. I carry well, but I carry best with my feet off the ground. What am I?

165. What is harder to catch the faster you run?

166. A boy at a carnival went to a booth run by a man who said, "If I can write your exact weight on this piece of paper then you have to give me $50, but if I cannot, I will pay you $50." The boy looked around and saw no scale so he agreed, thinking no matter what the carny writes he'll just say he weighs more or less. In the end the boy ended up paying the man $50. How did the man win the bet?

167. A man is trapped in a room. In the room there is a table, chair, 2 doors, and a small hole in the ceiling 12 inches in diameter. Behind one of the doors is an extremely hungry lion that hasn't eaten in a couple of days. Behind the other door is a glass tunnel that magnifies the sun creating temperatures so high that even opening the door could kill you. How does he escape?

168. This old one runs forever, but never moves at all. He hasn't any lungs or throat but still a mighty call. What is it?

169. Which word does not belong in the following list: Stop cop mop chop prop shop or crop?

170. I open to close but I close to open. I'm surrounded by water but I'm never soaking. What am I?

171. If you count 20 houses on your right going to the store and 20 houses on your left coming home, how many houses did you count?

172. I am not alive, but I grow; I don't have lungs but I need air; I don't have a mouth but water kills me. What am I?

173. I have a name that's not mine, and no one cares about me in their prime. People cry at my sight, and lie by me all day and night. What am I?

174. In what year did Christmas and New Year's Day fall in the same year?

175. If you toss a coin ten times and it lands heads up every time, what are the chances it will land heads up if you toss it again?

176. What is brown or silver, has a head and tail but no arms or legs?

177. Can you name three consecutive days without using the words Wednesday, Friday, or Sunday?

178. I have no wallet but I pay my way. I travel the world but in the corner I stay. What am I?

179. How can "L" be greater in size than "XL"?

180. A horse jumps over a castle and lands on a man, then the man disappears. How was this possible?

181. I am in everything and in nothing, what am I?

182. I do not eat food, but enjoy a light meal every day. What am I?

183. What fastens two people yet touches only one?

184. Decode these riddles;
A) 26 L of the A
B) 7 D of the W
C) 1000 Y in a M

185. Four hours ago, it was as long after 4 a.m. as it was before 4 p.m. the same day. What time is it now?

186. What is put on a table and cut, but never eaten?

187. Voiceless, it cries. Toothless, it bites. What is it?

188. What has one eye but cannot see?

189. What makes a loud noise when changing its jacket, becomes larger but weighs less?

190. I go around in circles, but always straight ahead, never complain, no matter where I am led. What am I?

191. It has a long neck, a name of a bird, feeds on cargo of ships and it's not alive. What is it?

192. What has to be broken before you can use it?

193. Divide 110 into two parts so that one number is a 150% of the other. What are the numbers?

194. What do you serve that you can't eat?

195. A father's child. A mother's child. No one's son. Who am I?

196. A tomato vine is 3 meters long. The bottom foot of the vine doesn't grow any tomatoes but the rest of the vine grows a tomato every 5 inches. How many vegetables can grow off the vine?

197. Which triangle will have a larger perimeter: 3,4,5 or 3,4,7?

198. I got it in a forest but didn't want it. Once I had it, I couldn't see it. The more I searched for it, the less I liked it. I took it home in my hand because I could not find it. What was it?

199. A man is asked what his daughters look like. He answers, "They are all blondes but two, all brunettes but two, and all redheads but two." How many daughters does he have?

200. What are the only 2 states that have their state name in their capital?

201. A boy has as many sisters as brothers, but each sister has only half as many sisters as brothers. How many brothers and sisters are there in the family?

202. We hurt without moving. We poison without touching. We bear the truth and the lies. We are not to be judged by our size. What are we?

203. What word looks the same upside down and backwards at the same time?

204. When I take five and add six, I get eleven, but when I take six and add seven, I get one. What am I?

205. There is a word in the English language in which the first two letters signify a male, the first three letters signify a female, the first four signify a great man, and the whole word, a great woman. What is the word?

206. Draw four rectangles on a piece of paper. Can you put nine x's in the four rectangles so that there is an uneven number of x's in each rectangle?

207. There are two doors and there is one guard for each door. One door leads to life and the other leads to death. You have only one question to ask and you can only ask one guard. One of the guards always tells the truth and the other always lies. What question would you ask to find out which door is the door to life?

208. You want to boil a two-minute egg. If you only have a three-minute timer (hourglass), a four-minute timer and a five-minute timer can you boil the egg for only two minutes?

209. I have ten or more daughters. I have less than ten daughters. I have at least one daughter. If only one of these statements is true, how many daughters do I have?

210. A great banquet was prepared for a Roman emperor and his courtiers. 22 Dormice, 40 Larks' Tongues, 30 Flamingos and 40 Roast Parrots were served. How many portions of Boiled Ostrich were served?

211. You have accidentally left out the plug and are attempting to fill the bath with both taps full on. The hot tap takes 6 minutes to fill the bath. The cold tap takes 2 minutes and the water empties through the plug hole in 4 minutes. In how many minutes will the bath be filled?

212. 0,1,2,3,4,5,6,7,8,9
Use the digits above once each only to compose two fractions which when added together equal 1.

213. Robert and David were preparing to have a water balloon fight. "Not fair" cried Robert, "You have 3 times as many as I do!" David said "Fine!" and gave Robert 10 more balloons. "Still not fair!" argued Robert, "You still have twice as many as I do." How many more balloons must David give Robert for them to have the same number?

214. There are a mix of red, green and yellow balls in a bag. The total number of balls is 60. There are four times as many red balls as green, and six more yellow balls than green balls. How many balls of each color are there?

215. Two bodies have I, though both joined in one. The more still I stand, the quicker I run. What am I?

216. What is it that given one, you'll have either two or none?

217. Large as a mountain, small as a pea, endlessly swimming in a waterless sea. What am I?

218. What types of words are these: madam, civic, eye, level?

219. 2 fathers and 2 sons go fishing. Each of them catches one fish. So why do they bring home only 3 fish?

220. Which is the word in English that has nine letters, and remains a word at each step even when you remove one letter from it, right up to a single letter remaining. List each letter as you remove them, along with the resulting word at each step.

221. Why is the number 8549176320 one of a kind?

222. $9 = 4$, $21 = 9$, $22 = 9$, $24 = 10$, $8 = 5$, $7 = 5$, $99 = 10$, $100 = 7$, $16 = ?$, $17 = ?$

223. John is 10 years old in 1870, but only 5 years old in 1875. How is this?

224. Which day is two days before the day after the day three days after the day before Tuesday?

225. Use math symbols to replace the question marks to make the following a valid equation:
12 ? 2 ? 7 ? 4 = 9

226. Who has four eyes but can never see?

227. How can you place a pencil on the floor so that no one can jump over it?

228. What language do people speak without saying a word?

229. You can easily touch me, but not see me. You can put me out but not away. What am I?

230. You put me in the ground when I am alive and dig me up when I am dead. What am I?

231. I am a mother and a father, but have never given birth. I'm rarely still, but I never wander. What am I?

232. Gary picked a book off the highest shelf in his room. On the spine, he read "How to Jog". The book had absolutely nothing to do with jogging. Why is that?

233. Brothers and sisters I have none but this man's father is my father's son. Who is the man?

234. You may enter, but you may not come in, I have space, but no room, I have keys, but open no lock. What am I?

235. What is wider than life itself, longer than forever, so simple it's complicated, travels but never leaves the spot, puts others in danger but no one gets hurt, and reaches to worlds unknown?

236. I build bridges of silver and crowns of gold. Who am I?

237. How can you add eight 8s to make 1000?

238. Two children were confused in their reckoning of the days of the week. They paused on their way to school to straighten matters out. "When the day after tomorrow is yesterday," said Sally, "then 'today' will be as far from Sunday as that day was which was 'today' when the day before yesterday was tomorrow. On which day of the week did this puzzling discussion occur?

239. A man is writing his will and he wants to leave everything he has to one of his two sons; whichever one is more dedicated. To decide which one will win his fortune he gives them each a car and tells them that whoever's car passes the finish line he has set up last will get everything he has. After a month of both sons refusing to cross the line they finally go to their uncle for advice. They both leave their uncles house in a hurry and race to the finish line as fast as they can. What advice did their uncle give?

240. How do you share 34 apples among 33 people?

241. There is a 5 gallon and a 3 gallon jar. How are you going to make the 5 gallon jar have 4 gallons in it using your items?

242. There is a party of 100 high-powered politicians. All of them are either honest or liars. You walk in knowing two things:
- At least one of them is honest.
- If you take any two politicians, at least one of them is a liar.
From this information, can you know how many are liars and how many are honest?

243. A very famous chemist was found murdered in his kitchen today. The police have narrowed it down to six suspects. They know it was a two-man job. Their names: Felice, Maxwell, Archibald, Nicolas, Jordan, and Xavier. A note was also found with the body: '26-3-58/28-27-57-16'.
Who are the killers?

244. A smooth dance, a ball sport, a place to stay, an Asian country, and a girl's name. What's her name?

245. To give me to someone I don't belong to is cowardly, but to take me is noble. I can be a game, but there are no winners. What am I?

246. There are several books on a bookshelf. If one book is the 4th from the left and 6th from the right, how many books are on the shelf?

247. How many letters are in the answer to this riddle?

248. Two men find an old gold coin and want to have a coin toss with it to decide who gets it. The only problem is the coin is heavier on one side so it comes up heads more than tails. What is a fair way for the men to toss the coin and decide who gets the coin?

249. If you have an 11 minute and a 13 minute hourglass, how can you accurately time 15 minutes?

250. This is an unusual paragraph. I'm curious as to just how quickly you can find out what is so unusual about it. It looks so ordinary and plain that you would think nothing was wrong with it. In fact, nothing is wrong with it! It is highly unusual though. Study it and think about it, but you still may not find anything odd. But if you work at it a bit, you might find out. Try to do so without any coaching.

251. Six glasses are in a row. The first three are filled with milk and the last three are empty. By moving only one glass, can you arrange them so that the full and the empty glasses alternate?

252. You put me in dry but then I get wet. The longer I stay in, the stronger it will get. What am I?

253. What are the next two letters in the following series and why? WATNTLITFS__

254. There is a brick of gold and a brick of iron in a boat (both 10-inch blocks). If they are both dropped into the water which will make the water level higher?

255. 500 is at my end and my start, yet 5 is at my heart. The first letter and the first number make me complete. My name is that of a king. Who am I?

256. When is 1500 plus 20 and 1600 minus 40 the same thing?

257. The more of me you have, the longer your life. The more of me you have, the less you have left. What am I?

258. John put a coin in a bottle and put a cork on the bottle and later managed to get the coin out without taking out the cork or breaking the bottle. How did he do it?

259. I'm the part of a bird that's not in the sky, I can swim in the ocean and remain dry. What am I?

260. Two boys, Trevor and Tyler, are running a 100-meter race. The first time they race Trevor beats Tyler by 5 meters. To make things fair, the next time they race Trevor stands 5 meters behind the starting line. Who wins the second race (assuming they run the same speed as the first race)?

261. 2 men catch 2 fish in 2 minutes. At this rate, how many men could catch 500 fish in 500 minutes?

262. What relation would your father's sister's sister-in-law be to you?

263. A man was born on January 1st, 23 B.C. and died January 2nd, 23 A.D. How old did he live to be?

264. What can you see but not hear?

265. You have two buckets: one with only white marbles and one with only black marbles. The two buckets have the same number of marbles. How can you rearrange the marbles to maximize your chances of grabbing a white marble from each?

266. You wear me every day but you never put me on. I will change colors if you leave me out too long. What am I?

267. A person has one lion, one lamb and a bundle of grass. He wants to cross a river but there is only one boat and it can't sustain the weight of more than two articles at a time. Also, he has to make sure that the lion doesn't eat the lamb and the lamb doesn't eat the grass. How will he get to the other side of the river with all three intact?

268. I can be long, or I can be short. I can be grown, or I can be bought. I can be painted or left bare. I can be round, or square. What am I?

269. If you eat me then my sender will eat you. What am I?

270. If you have 5 meters of wire fencing how do you create the largest area within the fence?

271. Too much for one, enough for two and nothing at all for three. What am I?

272. He makes shoes without leather, with all four elements put together. Fire, water, earth and air and every customer takes two pair. Who is he?

273. What walks all day on its head?

274. I have a little house in which I live all alone. My house has no doors or windows, and if I want to go out, I must break through the wall. What am I?

275. Thirty men and only two women, but they hold the most power. Dressed in black and white, they could fight for hours. Who are they?

276. A book has 500 pages:
The 1st page says "Exactly 1 page in this book is false."
The 2nd page says "Exactly 2 pages in this book are false."
...and so on...
The 500th page says "Exactly 500 pages in this book are false."
Can any of the pages be true?

277. A man hangs his hat and walks 500 yards with his eyes closed. He then turns around and shoots his hat with his pistol with his eyes still shut. How did he do this?

278. The 22nd and 24th Presidents of the United States have the same mother and father but are not brothers. How is this?

279. The day before yesterday Josh was 13 years old. Next year he will turn 16. How is this possible?

280. I build up castles.
I tear down mountains.
I make some men blind,
I help others to see.
What am I?

281. How long is the answer to this question?

282. The day before two days after the day before tomorrow is Saturday. What day is it today?

283. How can you make a fire with only one stick?

284. A smart landscaper is given the task of placing 4 trees so that they are all the same distance away from each other. How does he do this?

285. At school Joe has three friends: Tim, George and Paige. Two of them play football, two play tennis, and two play golf. The friend who doesn't play golf doesn't play tennis and the one who doesn't play football doesn't play golf. Girls don't play football. Which sports does each person play?

286. Christmas and New Year's Day occur exactly one week apart. So, a New Year's Day that occurs right after Christmas should be on the same day of the week. But in the year 2020 Christmas will occur on a Friday and New Year's Day on a Wednesday. Why is this?

287. You will always find me in the past. I can be created in the present, but the future can never taint me. What am I?

288. You have a cube made of 10 x 10 x 10 smaller cubes, for a total of 1000 smaller cubes. If you take off 1 layer of cubes, how many remain?

289. A man is doing some work on his home and goes to a hardware store. He goes up to the clerk and tells him what he wants. The clerk tells him that each one is $1. He tells the clerk he would like 5000 and he is charged only $4. What does he want?

290. A man can win a prize if he can shoot a can with a revolver. The revolver has six chambers but only has two bullets in it, both of them right next to each other. He can spin the revolver once and shoot the gun. If there was no bullet in that chamber, he has the option to either spin the chamber again or just shoot again. If the first shot is a blank, should the man ask for the revolver to be spun or should he choose to shoot again to maximize his chance of winning the prize?

291. Name an English word of more than 2 letters that both begins and ends with the letters 'he' (in that order). There are two possible correct answers.

292. What do these words have in common: age, blame, curb, dance, evidence, fence, gleam, harm, interest, jam, kiss, latch, motion, nest, order, part, quiz, rest, signal, trust, use, view, win, x-ray, yield, zone?

293. The ages of a father and son add up to 66. The father's age is the son's age reversed. How old could they be? There are three possible answers.

294. Two convicts are locked in a cell. There is an unbarred window high up in the cell. No matter if they stand on the bed or one on top of the other, they can't reach the window to escape. They then decide to tunnel out. However, they give up with the tunneling because it will take too long. Finally, one of the convicts figures out how to escape from the cell. What is his plan?

295. If two hours ago, it was as long after one o'clock in the afternoon as it was before one o'clock in the morning, what time would it be now?

296. A boy had just got out of the shower and was getting ready for his prom, shaved and there was going to be an after party. His mom and dad said be home for the next sunrise and he was home for the next sunrise but with a full-grown beard. How can this be?

297. My host thinks I'm an irritation, a bother, a pain. But he can't evict me, so here I will remain. Then one day I'm taken and ranked among my peers. Can you guess just what I am?

298. If seven people meet each other and each shakes hands only once with each of the others, how many handshakes will there have been?

299. Four men sat down to play. They played all night till break of day. They played for gold and not for fun. With separate scores for everyone. When they had come to square accounts, they all had made quite fair amounts. Can you the paradox explain, if no one lost, how all could gain?

300. Jenn gave Sue as many dollars as Sue had to start with. Sue then gave Jenn back as much as Jenn had left. Jenn then gave Sue back as many dollars as Sue now had, which left Jenn broke and gave Sue a total of $80.00. How much did Jenn and Sue have at the beginning of their exchange?

DIFFICULT RIDDLES ANSWERS

1. *A RIDDLE*

2. *A REFLECTION*

3. *FOOTSTEPS*

4. *A FART*

5. *BOOKKEEPER*

6. *STOP IMAGINING*

7. *QUEUE*

8. *A SECRET*

9. *HE IS PLAYING MONOPOLY*

10. *DOZENS*

11. *ARE YOU ASLEEP?*

12. *A WINDOW*

13. *HIS BREATH*

14. *THE LETTER M*

15. *A DOORBELL*

16. *IT'S CHEAPER TO TAKE TWO FRIENDS AT THE SAME TIME.
     IN THIS CASE, YOU WOULD ONLY BE BUYING THREE
     TICKETS, WHEREAS IF YOU TAKE THE SAME FRIEND TWICE
     YOU ARE BUYING FOUR TICKETS.*

17. *A HOLE*

18. *A SPONGE*

19. *THE EGG. DINOSAURS LAID EGGS BEFORE THERE WERE
     ANY CHICKENS.*

20. *WATER*

21. *A BALLOON*

22. *0*

23. *AN ANCHOR*

24. *A WORM*

25. *A BOXING RING*

26. *If they're square it's possible for the cover to slip down the hole (diagonally). A round manhole cannot fall down no matter which way it is rotated because it's width in any direction is greater than the opening on the hole.*

27. *Your tongue*

28. *The stars*

29. *Darkness*

30. *A teapot*

31. *Silence*

32. *Wholesome*

33. *Ton*

34. *A piano*

35. *A pig*

36. *Bananas (removed six letters)*

37. *A garbage truck*

38. *A* MAP

39. *W*ATER

40. *A* MATCH

41. *Y*OUR SHADOW

42. *B*EETLE

43. *A* DICTIONARY

44. *N*ONE – IT'S A HOLE

45. *N*ONE

46. *A* COAT OF PAINT

47. *E*DAM

48. *Y*OUR LEFT HAND

49. *F*EBRUARY

50. *I*TS LID

51. *T*HE HORIZON

52. *A* SHADOW

53. *A* MUSHROOM

54. *A* COLD

55. *A* DECK OF CARDS

56. THEY ARE BORN IN DIFFERENT TIME ZONES

57. *A* CARROT

58. *A* HORSE

59. REMOVE THE S

60. *A* QUESTION

61. *A* MEMORY

62. *50* PER CENT

63. WHITE. IT'S A POLAR BEAR.

64. AN ENVELOPE

65. SHE WAS WALKING

66. *6*

67. *THE THIRD ROOM. LIONS THAT HAVEN'T EATEN IN THREE YEARS ARE DEAD.*

68. *A NEWSPAPER*

69. *A SNOWFLAKE*

70. *THE BRAIN*

71. *YOU*

72. *A RIVER*

73. *A PENCIL*

74. *A CANDLE*

75. *A HOUSEFLY*

76. *YOUR AGE*

77. *THERE AREN'T ANY PENGUINS IN THE ARCTIC.*

78. *IT ISN'T RAINING OUTSIDE.*

79. *A FENCE*

80. *THE SUN*

81. *IT IS A FAKE. NO COIN CAN SAY BC.*

82. *THERE AREN'T ANY STAIRS.*

83. *BECAUSE ITS PARENTS WERE IN A JAM.*

84. *A JOKE*

85. *AN ELEVATOR*

86. *A PENDULUM*

87. *AN ADDRESS*

88. *YOUR NAME*

89. *A SKULL*

90. *A CLOCK*

91. *1,2 AND 3*

92. *A RIVER*

93. *HE WAS A PRIEST*

94. *I'M YOUR BRAIN*

95. *ADVICE*

96. *AN ONION*

97. *AN ICEBERG*

98. *AN ECHO*

99. *NORTH*

100. *A BOTTLE*

FIENDISH RIDDLES ANSWERS

101. *They are part of a set of triplets.*

102. *Time and tide wait for no man.*

103. *You don't knock on your own hotel door and the man did.*

104. *Stand back to back*

105. *The alphabet*

106. *NOON*

107. *An eye*

108. *Birds of a feather flock together.*

109. *Eat and Ate*

110. *A map*

111. *A turtle*

112. *A bell*

113. *E N T. THEY REPRESENT THE FIRST LETTER WHEN WRITING THE NUMBERS ONE THRU TEN.*

114. *A ROLLING STONE GATHERS NO MOSS.*

115. *SPARSELY*

116. *A COFFIN*

117. *AN EGG*

118. *A SHIRT*

119. *WHEAT, HEAT, EAT, TEA*

120. *A FISH*

121. *VOWELS*

122. *TOOTHPASTE*

123. *THE LETTERS I & S*

124. *THE BEGGAR WAS A WOMAN.*

125. *A KANGAROO*

126. *A SHOE*

127. A DOUGHNUT

*128. O*NE – JUST ME

*129. S*HE KICKED IT TEN FEET IN THE AIR

*130. N*EVER BECAUSE THE BOAT WILL RISE WITH THE TIDE.

131. B IS A DAUGHTER

*132. L*IGHT

*133. C*ORN ON THE COB

134. A FAN

*135. P*RISON

*136. D*ARKNESS

*137. T*IME

*138. P*EA

*139. P*LATES AND CUTLERY

*140. S*AWDUST

141. 0

142. 199-99

143. BECAUSE WHEN YOU FIND IT, YOU STOP LOOKING.

144. A BAR OF SOAP

145. A SNOWMAN

146. TRAFFIC LIGHTS

147. ADD THE LETTER 'G' AND IT'S 'GONE'

148. ONE - THE DRIVER

149. A CENTIPEDE ON ITS BACK

150. THEY ARE ALL BEDS

151. HE WAS INSIDE CLEANING WINDOWS

152. CARPET

153. DARKNESS

154. YOUR VOICE

155. VEGETABLE

156. A TELEPHONE

157. *Golf*

158. *They will be the same distance from London.*

159. *Just one*

160. *None. They flew off.*

161. *95. Dividing by 1/2 is the same as multiplying by 2. So, 40 x 2 + 15 = 95.*

162. *He is a pilot in the cabin of the airplane.*

163. *Human skin*

164. *Wheelbarrow*

165. *Your breath*

166. *The man did exactly as he said he would and wrote "your exact weight" on the paper.*

167. *He waits until it is night (he can tell through the hole in the ceiling) then leaves through the glass tunnel.*

168. *A waterfall*

169. OR

170. A DRAWBRIDGE

171. 20 - THEY ARE THE SAME HOUSES

172. FIRE

173. A TOMBSTONE

174. EVERY YEAR

175. THERE'S A 50 PERCENT CHANCE IT WILL LAND HEADS UP. THE FINAL COIN TOSS IS INDEPENDENT OF THE FIRST TEN TOSSES.

176. A COIN

177. YESTERDAY, TODAY, AND TOMORROW

178. A STAMP

179. ROMAN NUMERALS

180. IT IS A CHESS GAME.

181. THE LETTER T

182. A PLANT

183. A WEDDING RING

184. A) 26 LETTERS OF THE ALPHABET
  B) 7 DAYS OF THE WEEK
  C) 1000 YEARS IN A MILLENNIUM

185. 2 P.M. THE HALFWAY POINT BETWEEN 4 A.M. AND 4 P.M. IS 10 A.M., BUT THAT WAS 4 HOURS AGO. THUS, 10 A.M. + 4 HOURS = 2 P.M.

186. A PACK OF CARDS

187. THE WIND

188. A NEEDLE

189. POPCORN

190. WHEEL

191. CRANE

192. AN EGG

193. THE NUMBERS ARE 44 AND 66.

194. A TENNIS BALL

195. A DAUGHTER

196. THE VINE WON'T GROW ANY VEGETABLES, A TOMATO IS A FRUIT. BUT THE VINE WILL GROW 21 TOMATOES.

197. 3,4 AND 5 BECAUSE 3,4 AND 7 DOESN'T MAKE A TRIANGLE.

198. A SPLINTER

199. THREE: ONE BLONDE, ONE BRUNETTE AND ONE REDHEAD.

200. OKLAHOMA CITY AND INDIANAPOLIS

201. FOUR BROTHERS AND THREE SISTERS

202. WORDS

203. SWIMS

204. A CLOCK

205. HEROINE

206. DRAW ONE LARGE RECTANGLE. THEN DRAW THE THREE SMALLER RECTANGLES WITHIN THE LARGE RECTANGLE. PLACE THREE X'S IN EACH SMALL RECTANGLE. THERE WILL BE NINE X'S IN THE LARGE RECTANGLE.

207. YOU WOULD ASK: "IF I WERE TO ASK THE OTHER GUARD WHICH DOOR LEADS TO LIFE, WHAT WOULD HE SAY?" THE GUARD THAT TELLS THE TRUTH KNOWS THAT THE OTHER GUARD WOULD LIE. SO HE TELLS THE TRUTH AND POINTS TO THE DOOR THAT LEADS TO DEATH. THE GUARD THAT LIES KNOWS THAT THE OTHER GUARD WOULD TELL THE TRUTH. SO HE LIES AND POINTS TO THE DOOR THAT LEADS TO DEATH. BOTH GUARDS POINT TO THE DEATH DOOR.

208. *ONCE THE WATER IS BOILING, TURN THE THREE-MINUTE TIMER AND FIVE-MINUTE TIMER OVER. WHEN THE THREE-MINUTE TIMER RUNS OUT, PUT THE EGG IN THE BOILING WATER. WHEN THE FIVE-MINUTE TIMER RUNS OUT, TWO MINUTES HAVE ELAPSED AND IT IS TIME TO TAKE THE EGG OUT OF THE WATER. YOU DON'T NEED THE FOUR-MINUTE TIMER FOR THIS RIDDLE.*

209. *IF I HAVE ANY DAUGHTERS, THERE WILL ALWAYS BE TWO STATEMENTS WHICH ARE TRUE. THEREFORE, I HAVE NO DAUGHTERS.*

210. *EACH VOWEL IS WORTH 2 AND EACH CONSONANT 4, SO DORMICE GIVES 22, ETC.*

211. *2 MINUTES 24 SECONDS. FOR EXAMPLE TAKE A 12 GALLON BATH TUB. IF THE HOT TAP TAKES 6 MINUTES TO FILL THE BATH ITS RATE IS TWO GALLONS A MINUTE. THE COLD TAP TAKES TWO MINUTES, SO ITS RATE IS 6 GALLONS A MINUTE. THE PLUG HOLE EMPTIES THE BATH IN FOUR MINUTES AT A RATE OF 3 GALLONS A MINUTE. SO THE RATE OF FILLING THE BATH IS 2+6-3=5 GALLONS PER MINUTE. SO THE 12 GALLON BATH IS FILLED IN 2 MINUTES 24 SECONDS.*

212. *35/70 + 148/296 = 1*

213. *DAVID MUST GIVE ROBERT ANOTHER 20 WATER BALLOONS, GIVING THEM EACH 60. ROBERT STARTED WITH 30 WATER BALLOONS AND DAVID WITH 90.*

214. *THERE ARE 15 YELLOW BALLS, 36 RED BALLS AND 9 GREEN BALLS.*

215. *AN HOURGLASS*

216. *A CHOICE*

217. *ASTEROIDS*

218. *THEY ARE PALINDROMES; THEY READ THE SAME BOTH WAYS.*

219. *BECAUSE THE FISHING GROUP COMPRISES A GRANDFATHER, HIS SON, AND HIS GRANDSON - HENCE JUST THREE PEOPLE.*

220. *'STARTLING' IS THE WORD. BEGIN BY REMOVING 'L', WHICH MAKES IT 'STARTING', THEN TAKE AWAY THE 'T', MAKING IT 'STARING', AND SO ON - STRING; STING; SING; SIN; IN; AND, I.*

221. ALL THE NUMBERS (0-9) APPEAR ONLY ONCE AND ALL IN ALPHABETICAL ORDER.

222. 16 = 7 AND 17 = 9. THE NUMBER OF LETTERS IN THE SPELLING OF 16 (SIXTEEN) IS 7 AND THAT OF 17 (SEVENTEEN) IS 9.

223. JOHN WAS BORN IN 1880 BC.

224. WEDNESDAY

225. 12 DIVIDED BY 2 + 7 - 4 = 9

226. MISSISSIPPI

227. PLACE IT AGAINST A WALL.

228. BODY LANGUAGE

229. YOUR BACK

230. A PLANT

231. A TREE

232. THE BOOK GARY PICKED UP WAS ONE OF A SET OF ENCYCLOPEDIAS; HE HAD PICKED UP THE VOLUME CONTAINING ENTRIES BEGINNING WITH THE LETTERS "HOW" THROUGH THE LETTERS "JOG".

233. THE MAN IS THE RIDDLE TELLER'S SON.

234. A COMPUTER

235. YOUR IMAGINATION

236. A DENTIST

237. 888 + 88 + 8 + 8 + 8 = 1000

238. THE TWO CHILDREN WERE SO BEFOGGED OVER THE CALENDAR THAT THEY HAD STARTED ON THEIR WAY TO SCHOOL ON SUNDAY MORNING!

239. THEIR UNCLE TOLD THEM TO SWITCH CARS. IF THEY SWITCH CARS THEY ARE DRIVING THEIR BROTHER'S CAR AND IF THEY DRIVE THEIR BROTHER'S CAR PAST THE FINISH LINE FIRST, THEIR CAR WILL BE LAST AND THEY WILL WIN.

240. MAKE APPLE SAUCE

241. *You fill the five gallon box up and pour it into the 3 gallon one. Then dump the 3 gallons out and pour what was left in the 5 gallon box into the 3 gallon one so that you have 2 gallons in the 3 gallon box. Then fill the 5 gallon one up and pour it into the 3 gallon one to fill it up. Now you have 4 gallons in the 5 gallon box.*

242. *Yes, from the information you know 1 is honest and 99 are liars. One of them is honest satisfying the first piece of information. Then if you take the honest man and any other politician, the other politician must be a liar to satisfy the second piece of information, 'If you take any two politicians, at least one of them is a liar.' So, 99 are liars.*

243. *Felice and Nicholas are the murderers. The numbers correspond to atomic numbers on the periodic table of elements: 'Fe-Li-Ce/Ni-Co-La-S'.*

244. *Juliet, all of the listed things describe a part of the NATO phonetic alphabet: Foxtrot, golf, hotel, India, and finally Juliet.*

245. **Blame**

246. 9

247. **Four** *(this is the only number that makes the statement true).*

248. **They just have to flip it twice. They call the first toss either heads or tails, then the next toss they automatically pick the opposite (i.e. if one man calls heads on the first flip, he automatically picks tails on the second and vice versa). If they both win one toss (a tie) out of the two, they just have to repeat until one of them wins both tosses.**

249. **Start both hourglasses then when the 11-minute hourglass has finished immediately flip it again. When the 13-minute hourglass runs out the 11-minute hourglass will have 9 minutes left, so flip it and it will last another 2 minutes, 13 minutes + 2 minutes = 15 minutes.**

250. **The letter E, which is the most common letter used in the English language, does not appear in the paragraph.**

251. POUR THE SECOND GLASS OF MILK INTO THE FIFTH EMPTY GLASS.

252. A TEABAG

253. AW- THE LETTERS ARE THE BEGINNING LETTERS OF EACH OF THE WORDS IN THE SENTENCE.

254. THE IRON WILL MAKE THE WATER LEVEL HIGHER. IN THE BOAT THEY HAVE A LARGER EFFECT ON THE WATER LEVEL (RAISE THE WATER LEVEL) AND THEN WHEN THEY ARE DROPPED INTO THE WATER THE LIGHTER ONE (IRON) WILL MAKE THE WATER LEVEL DROP LESS BECAUSE IT IS LIGHTER AND HAS LESS EFFECT ON THE WATER FROM THE BOAT BUT DISPLACES THE SAME AMOUNT OF WATER AS THE GOLD WHEN DROPPED INTO THE WATER.

255. DAVID. D=500, V=5, AND I=1 (THE FIRST NUMBER). 'A' IS THE FIRST LETTER OF THE ALPHABET.

256. 24 HOUR CLOCK

257. HEARTBEATS

258. HE PUSHED THE CORK INTO THE BOTTLE.

259. A SHADOW

260. *Trevor wins again. In the first race Trevor ran 100 meters in the time it took Tyler to run 95 meters. So in the second race when Tyler is at the 95 meter mark Trevor will also be there (since 100 - 5 = 95). Since Trevor is faster he will pass Tyler in the last 5 meters of the race.*

261. *2 men*

262. *Your mother*

263. *There is no year 0 so you can add 23 to 23 but you must subtract one to take year 0 out of consideration: 23 + 23 - 1 = 45 years old.*

264. *Light*

265. *Put a single white marble in one bucket and put the rest of the white marbles and all of the black marbles in the other. This makes your odds about 75 percent for grabbing two white marbles.*

266. *Skin*

267. TAKE THE LAMB ACROSS, THEN THE BUNDLE OF GRASS. TAKE THE LAMB BACK ACROSS AND THEN TAKE THE LION ACROSS. THEN TAKE THE LAMB BACK ACROSS AND THEY ARE ALL UNHARMED.

268. FINGERNAILS

269. A FISH HOOK

270. YOU BUILD A FENCE AROUND YOURSELF AND DECLARE YOURSELF TO BE ON THE OUTSIDE.

271. A SECRET

272. BLACKSMITH

273. A NAIL IN A HORSESHOE

274. A CHICK IN AN EGG

275. THEY ARE CHESS PIECES

276. YES, THE 499TH PAGE IS TRUE. IT SAYS "EXACTLY 499 PAGES IN THIS BOOK ARE FALSE." WITH THIS PAGE TRUE, THE OTHER 499 PAGES ARE FALSE, FULFILLING THE STATEMENT.

277. *He hangs his hat on the barrel of his gun.*

278. *It is the same man, Grover Cleveland, who served two terms, which weren't consecutive.*

279. *You're speaking on January 1st. On December 30th, he was 13. The next day was his 14th birthday. He's turning 15 on the last day of THIS year, so he's turning 16 on the last day of next year.*

280. *Sand*

281. *How long*

282. *A Friday*

283. *Make sure it is a matchstick.*

284. *He puts three trees into a triangle then one on a hill in the middle (this forms a tetrahedron).*

285. *George and Tim play all three sports and Paige plays none.*

286. In 2020 New Year's occurs on January 1st, 2020 and Christmas on December 25th, 2020. These dates are 51 weeks and 2 days apart, not one week apart (during the year New Year's occurs before Christmas).

287. History

288. The remaining cube will be 8 x 8 x 8. This will be 512. A layer is taken from all sides of the cube, so it would reduce the dimensions by two, not one.

289. House numbers

290. He should shoot again. If it is spun again there is a 2/6 chance he will shoot the can. There are four possible spots that don't have bullets and only one is followed by a bullet. This means that the chance is only 1/4 that he will shoot the can if he doesn't spin it.

291. Headache or Heartache

292. All the words can be used as both nouns and verbs.

293. 51 and 15, 42 and 24, 60 and 06

294. His plan is to dig the tunnel and pile up the dirt to climb up to the window to escape.

295. Nine o'clock. Since there are twelve hours between the two times, and half of that time equals six, then the halfway mark would have to be seven o'clock. If it were seven o'clock two hours ago, the time would now be nine o'clock.

296. He lives in Alaska and sunrises are every six months.

297. I am a Pearl.

298. Twenty one

299. The men were musicians.

300. Jenn had $50 and Sue had $30.

One Last Thing

If you have enjoyed this book, I would love you to write a review of it on Amazon. It is really useful feedback as well as untold encouragement to the author.

Any remarks are highly appreciated, so if you have any comments, or suggestions for improvements to this publication, or for other books, I would love to hear from you.

You can contact me at
m.prefontaine2@gmail.com

All your input is greatly valued, and the books have already been revised and improved as a result of helpful suggestions from readers.

Thank you.

Made in the USA
Lexington, KY
17 December 2019